Cancer

The Whispered Word

by
Judy Harris Swenson
and Roxane Brown Kunz

Illustrated by
Jeanette Swofford

DILLON PRESS, INC.
MINNEAPOLIS, MINNESOTA 55415

This book is dedicated to Dr. William L. Bunting and the many other caring professionals and volunteers who dedicate their talent, skill, time, and compassion to helping those who must deal with the disease of cancer.

Library of Congress Cataloging in Publication Data

Swenson, Judy Harris.
   Cancer, the whispered word.

   Summary: Presents information about cancer, emphasizing those things of particular interest to children and describing how the disease affects family members.
   1. Cancer—Juvenile literature. [1. Cancer]
I. Kunz, Roxane Brown. II. Title.
RC263.S98   1985   616.99'4   85-6983
ISBN 0-87518-310-7

© 1986 by Dillon Press, Inc. All rights reserved

Dillon Press, Inc., 242 Portland Avenue South
Minneapolis, Minnesota 55415

Printed in the United States of America
   2 3 4 5 6 7 8 9 10 94 93 92 91 90 89 88 87 86

Acknowledgments

We wish to thank Jo Elizabeth Ridenour, RN, Director of Nurses at Maricopa Medical Center, and Cathy Milton, RN, Oncology Nurse, Maricopa Medical Center, for their expertise in evaluating and advising us on this book.

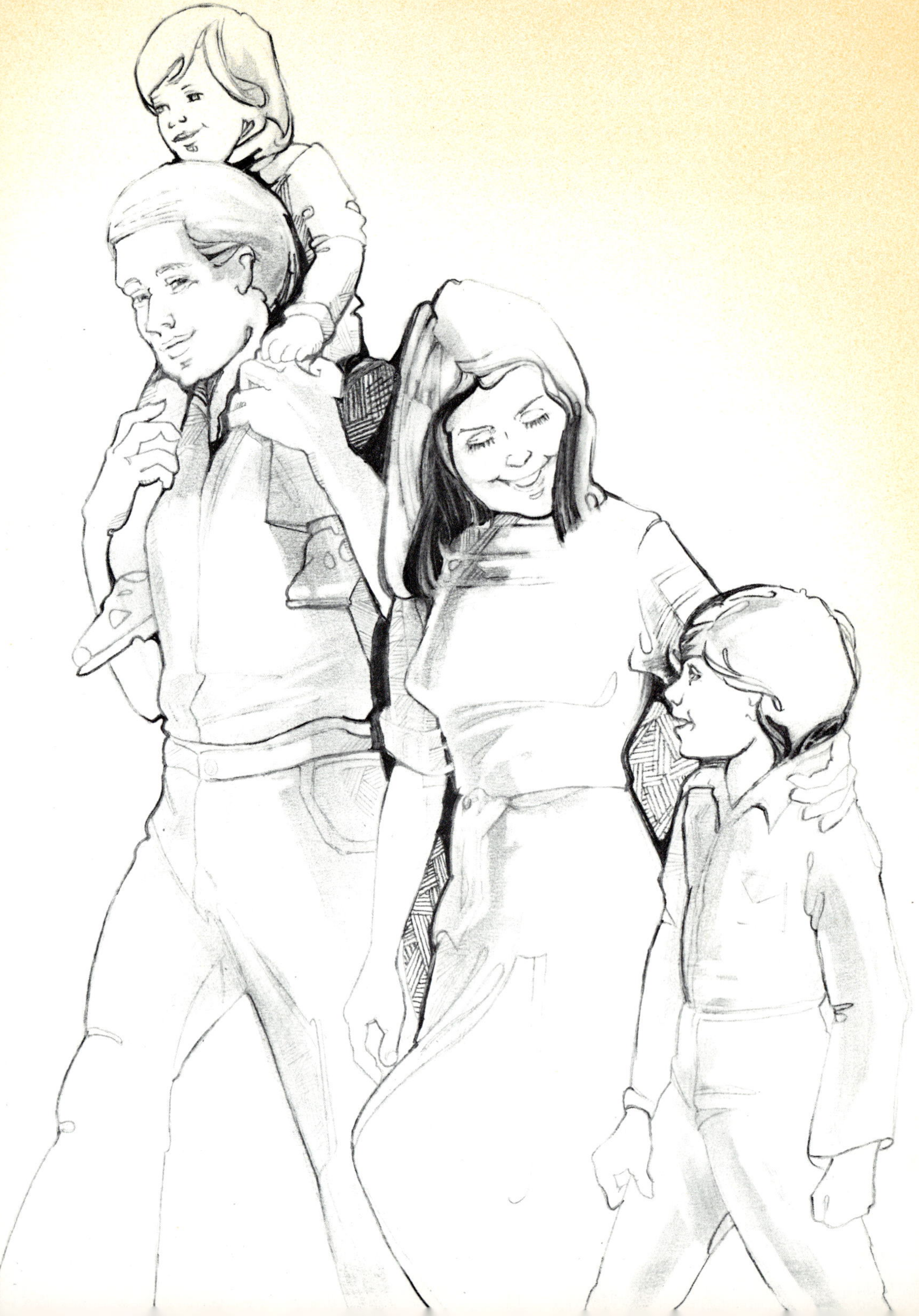

Mom has always been a very busy person. When she would get a cold she would say, "Oh Bill, I don't have time to be sick. I have to keep my family on their toes."

Well, Mom did get sick. . .real sick. I never thought she would, but this is what happened.

One day last spring, Mom said that she was going to the doctor. We were really surprised. Mom didn't look sick. She didn't even have a sniffle. "Oh, I'm not sick," Mom said. "I feel fine, but I have a small lump that won't go away. I'm just going to have a checkup."

Now that was smart! No one should be too busy to have a checkup. What could be easier?

Going for a checkup was a good idea, although things did not turn out to be so simple for Mom. The doctor didn't like what he saw. He wanted Mom to go to the hospital for an **operation**. Her lump needed to be removed. It would be looked at under a **microscope** with special equipment. This kind of simple operation is called a **biopsy**. A biopsy tells the doctor if a lump is dangerous to good health.

I was worried about Mom's lump because I knew it could be serious. Not long ago our class had a health lesson about lumps and bruises from our school nurse. We learned that everyone's body is made up of **cells**. Sometimes

Cancer Cells   Normal Cells

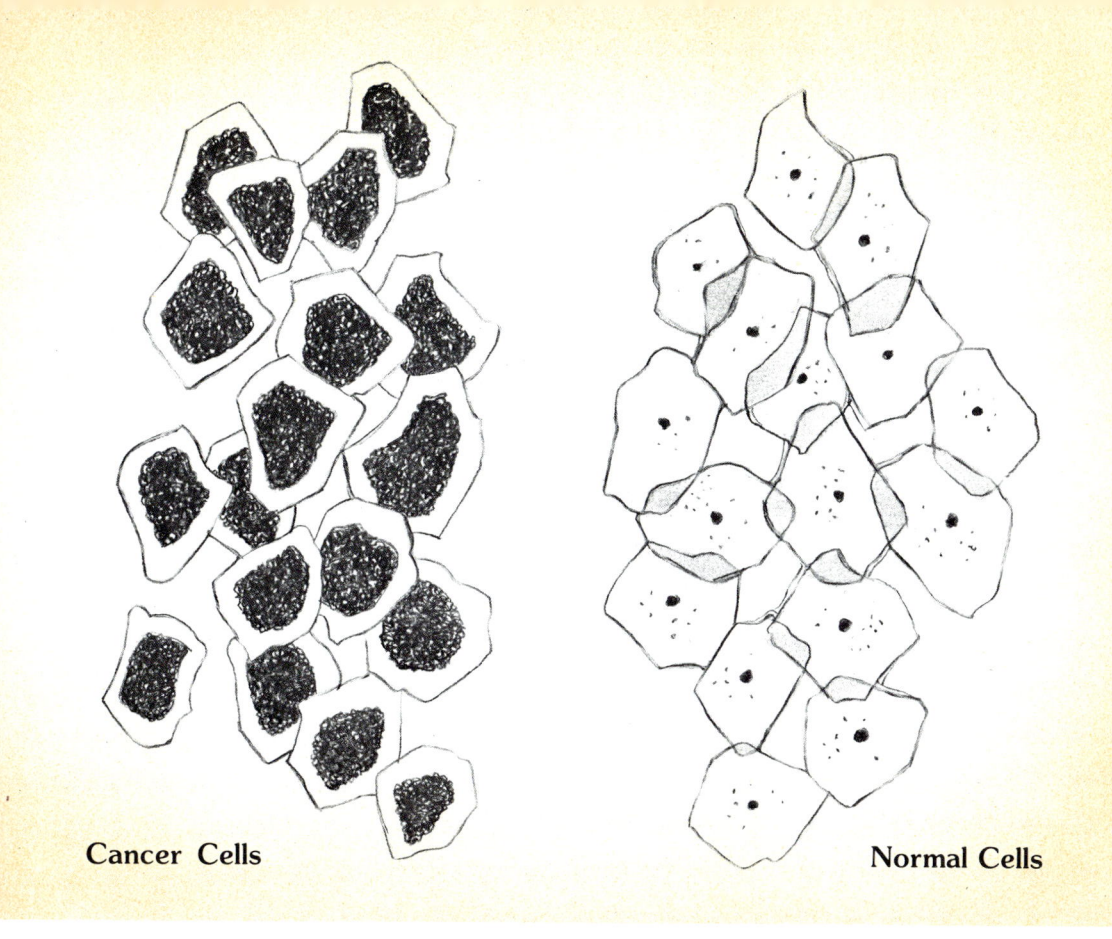

something goes wrong with the cells. They may grow and spread too fast.

Some cells that grow too quickly destroy healthy cells. These rapidly growing cells are caused by a **disease** called **cancer**. Cancer cells can spread to other parts of the body and can get into the blood.

Cells that grow too fast can build up until they form a lump or **tumor**. Most tumors are **benign**. That means there is no disease in those cells. Benign lumps do not spread to other parts of the body.

Tumors that contain cancer cells are **malignant**. A malignant tumor is dangerous because the cancer cells it contains can spread to other parts of the body. You can imagine that I was very nervous, wondering if Mom had cancer.

I could tell that Mom was nervous, too. She was trying not to show it, but she just wasn't herself. One day she started to stuff a load of dirty clothes into the dishwasher.

Mom called Grandma Libby and talked to her for a long time. I knew Grandma would come to stay with us while Mom was in the hospital. After all, someone had to take care of my little brother, Harry.

Sure enough, Monday morning Grandma Libby arrived from L.A. I love having Grandma visit. She's a great cook and plays neat games with me.

I could take care of myself, but Harry is a problem. He is a two-year-old Munchkin Mischief Maker. Grandma had a big job ahead of her.

The next day Mom headed for the hospital. "Wow," Mom joked, "this is like going on a vacation. No cooking, cleaning, washing dishes, or shopping. I just might get used to this."

We all waved good-bye as Mom and Dad drove away. A few minutes later they came back. I knew they would. Mom had forgotten her suitcase. I thought that she must really be worried.

At the hospital a special doctor called a **surgeon** did an operation to remove Mom's tumor. Mom had been given some medicine so that she would sleep and feel no pain. She would wake up when the operation was over. The cells of the tumor had to be looked at closely to see if they were malignant or benign. This was done in a room known as a **laboratory**.

Dad came home late the night of Mom's operation. I heard Grandma and Dad talking. Grandma whispered the word *cancer*.

Cancer! My mom had cancer. My heart pounded, and my hands began to sweat. I was scared.

"Come here, Bill," Dad called softly. He knew I was still up and listening at the door. (Harry was sound asleep.) "Let's have a cup of hot chocolate and talk about what has happened."

Dad brought two mugs of hot chocolate into the room and set them on the coffee table. Now I knew for sure the news was not good. We can never have drinks in the living room.

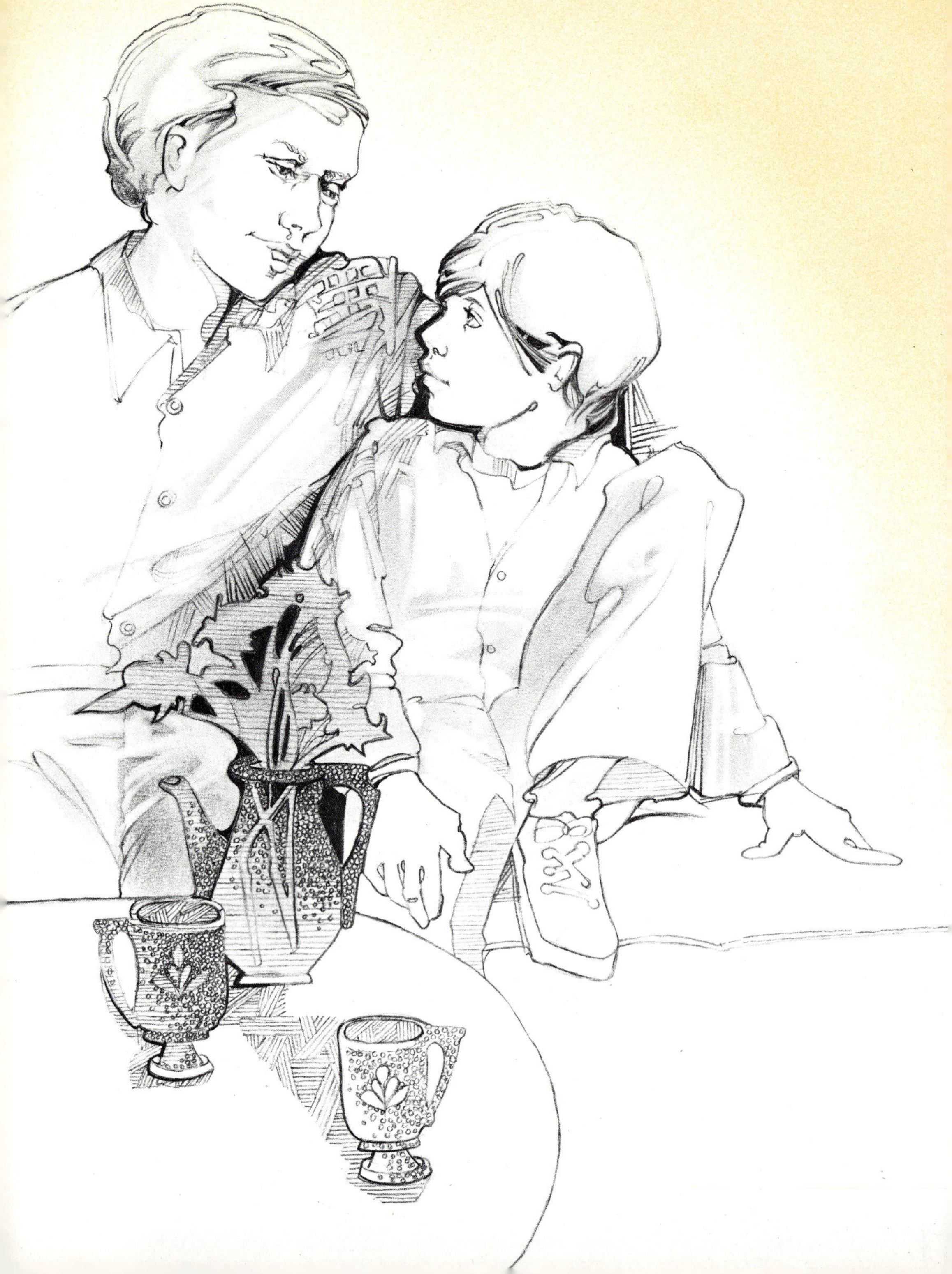

Dad sat down next to me. "Bill," he said, "Mom has cancer."

When I heard the word cancer again, I squeezed my fists and blinked my eyes hard.

Dad put his arm around my shoulders. "I know you will have many questions," he said. "I'll try to answer them for you."

I was still scared. I started to cry. There had been a movie on T.V. about a football player with cancer. He died. I asked Dad if Mom would die, too. Dad said that this was one question no one could answer for sure. Sometimes cancer can be **cured**. It all depends on how soon it is discovered and what can be done for it. There are many different kinds of cancer, and some are easier to control than others.

Mom had found out about her cancer early. She was getting good medical care. The doctor told Dad that he thought she would get well. Everyone was doing the best they could.

My mind was full of questions. Dad understood and didn't make me wait until morning to ask them. There were things about cancer that he didn't know either. We got out our encyclopedia for some information.

We found out that many things in our world are believed to cause cancer. They are called **carcinogens**. When carcinogens attack healthy cells, they sometimes cause one cell to become diseased. This is the beginning of cancer.

Dad said it is important to know that the same carcinogens do not cause cancer in everyone. Everyone's body reacts differently, and what causes cancer in one person will not necessarily cause cancer in someone else.

I also learned that there are two main groups of carcinogens that can cause cancer in people—some **chemicals** and certain types of **radiation**. Saccharin, which is found in diet foods, and tobacco are chemical carcinogens. Unclean air and polluted water may also contain chemical carcinogens. The sun and x-rays contain radiation carcinogens. Too much sun and too many x-rays are known to cause cancer in people.

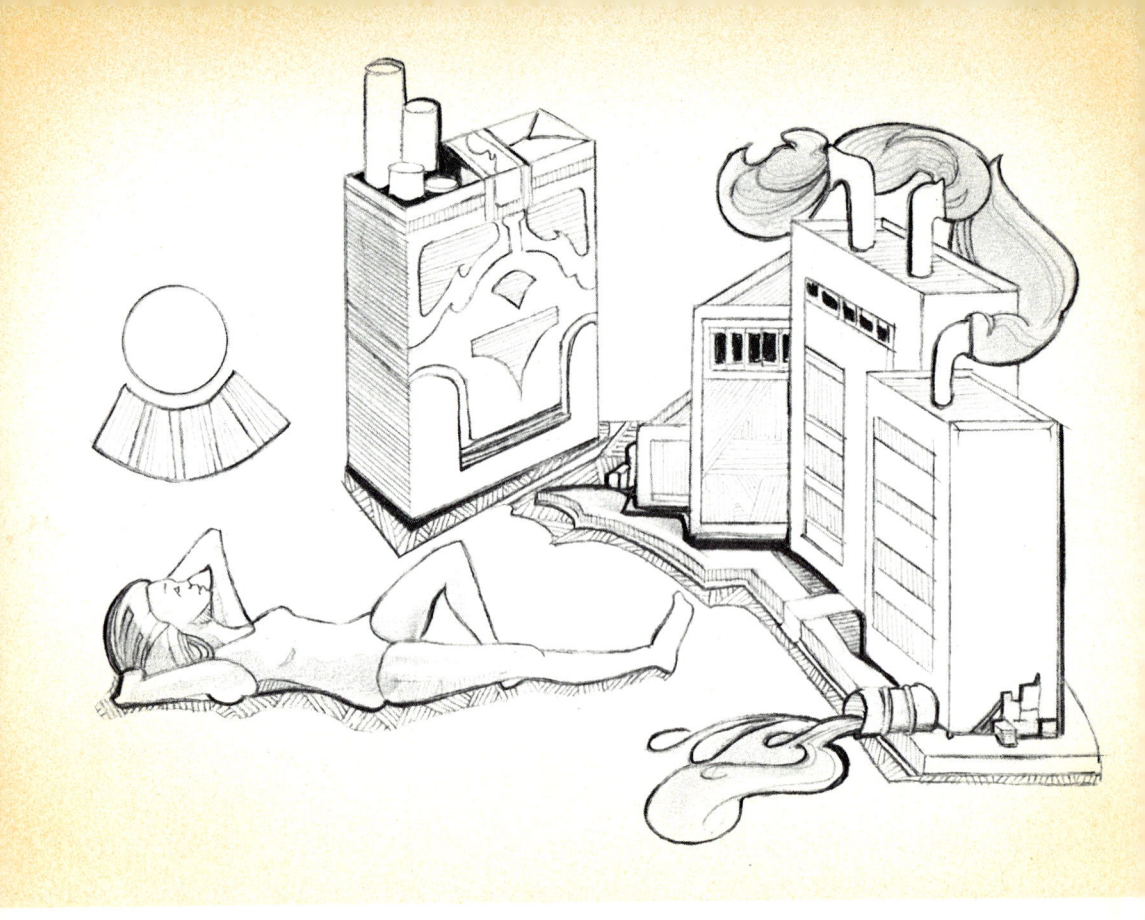

    Dad said that one way we can take care of our bodies is to try to stay away from carcinogens. I can read the warning labels on food and not use tobacco. A hat and sunscreen will help to protect my skin when I am in the sun.

16

When Dad tucked me in bed, I still had one more question. "Dad," I whispered, "can I catch Mom's cancer?" I sure felt better when he told me no. Cancer is not **contagious** like a cold.

A few days later Mom came home from the hospital. Even though the tumor was gone, the doctor told her that she still might have cancer cells in her body. There are several ways cancer can be treated. Mom began going to the hospital as an **outpatient** for her treatments. Monday through Friday Mom was treated with radiation. Some days she took **chemotherapy**. These treatments were to try and stop the cancerous cells from spreading.

Mom said that radiation was almost like having an x-ray. It didn't hurt. Chemotherapy meant that she took special medicine or drugs to fight the cancer cells in her body. Sometimes Mom was given the chemotherapy through a needle, and sometimes she swallowed a pill.

I hoped Mom's treatments would help her to get well. The doctor told Dad that if the bad cells stopped growing, Mom would be in **remission**. If Mom's cancer could not be stopped, the word **terminal** might be used. Terminal would mean that she wasn't getting well.

Dad explained to me that cancer treatments are not the same for everyone. People's bodies

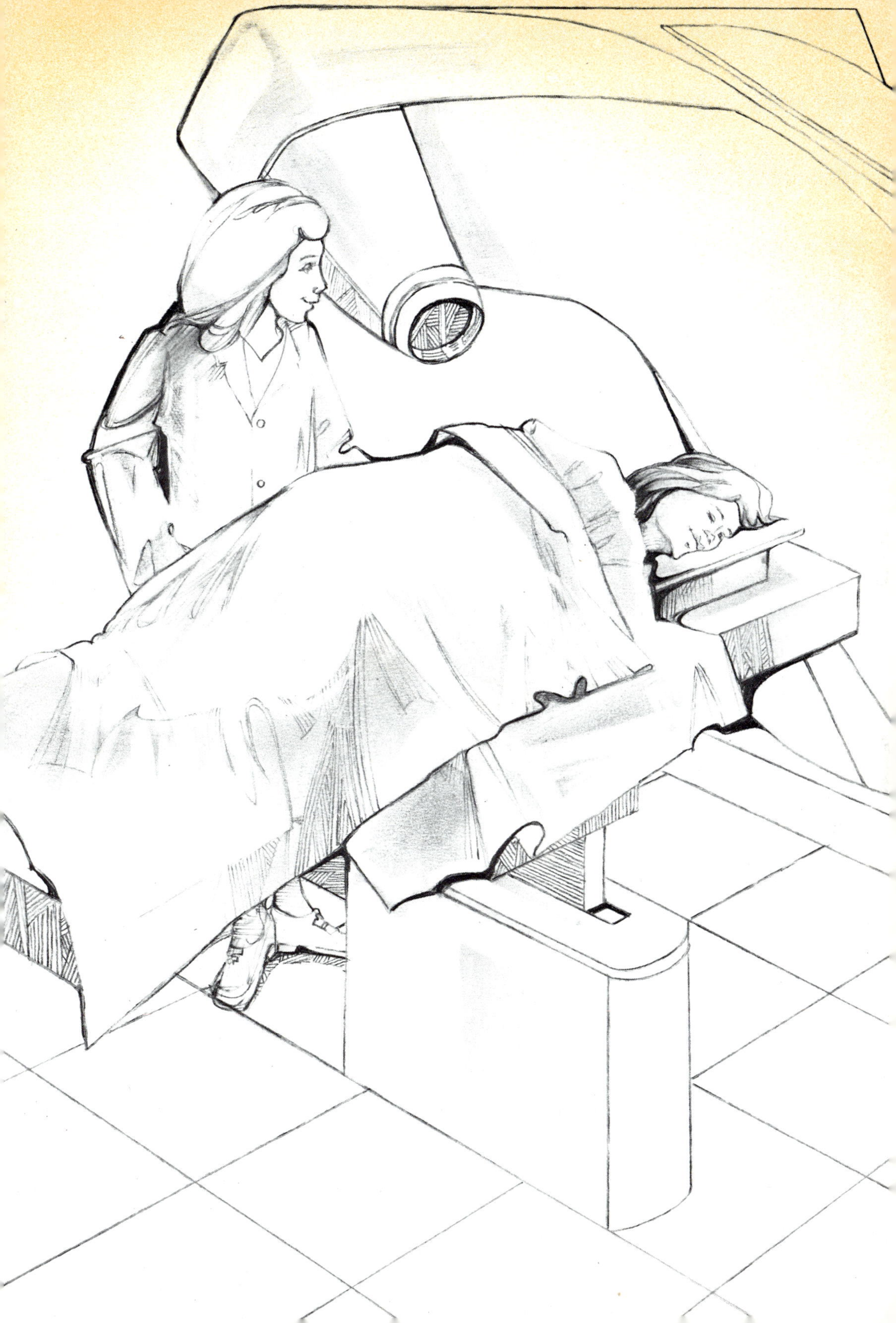

can react differently to cancer treatments. Mom's cancer treatments made her feel sick to her stomach. Sometimes she didn't want to eat. I felt sad when she couldn't eat dinner with us.

I felt even worse when Mom's treatments began to make her lose most of her beautiful, shiny hair. I didn't want my friends to see her bald head. I knew these changes made Mom feel bad, too. When my friends came over, she wore a wig or a little scarf.

Even with Mom at home, things were not the same. Mom was often tired. She needed her rest and took naps everyday, just like Harry. Grandma had to go back to her own home, so Dad and

I took over some of the jobs Mom usually did.

At first helping with the laundry and cleaning was fun. But one day I put Dad's red sweatshirt in with my white underwear when I was doing the wash. My underwear all turned pink! Enough was enough!

Life at our house wasn't fun anymore. I didn't want my Mom to be sick, and I was tired of doing her jobs. One day I had special chores to do, and Mom asked me to be home early. Some of the guys asked me to play soccer. I really wanted to play, and that is exactly what I did.

Gee, did I kick that soccer ball around. Still, the harder I kicked the more I thought about

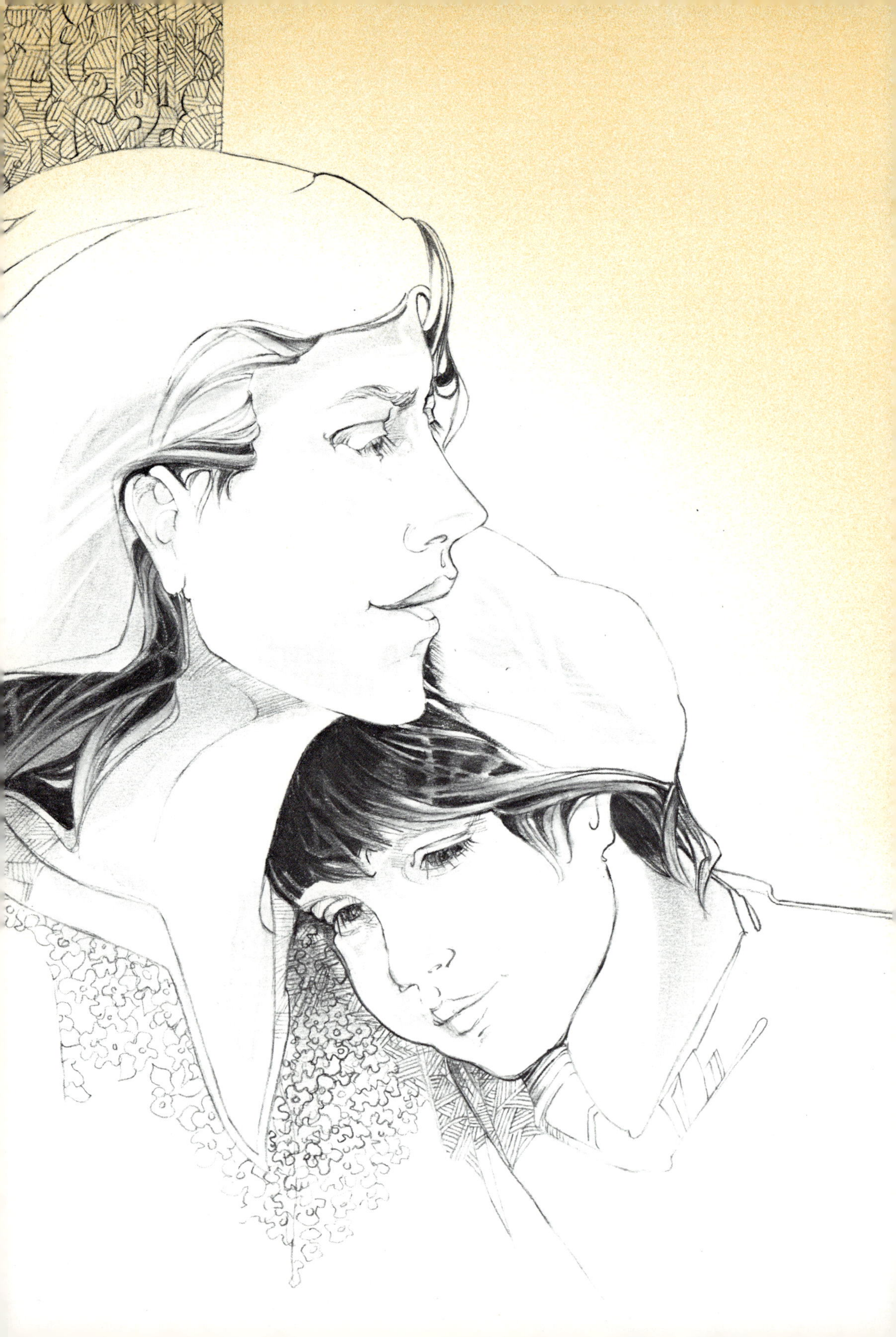

Mom and her cancer. Cancer had become a real drag. I was angry with Mom for being sick. Things had changed so much that I didn't even want to go home. Then I felt terrible. Mom was so special, and I loved her very much. I knew it wasn't her fault that she was sick. I had let her down. Why was I acting like this?

Mom was waiting for me when I got home. She said that she was glad I was safe. I began to cry and told her that I was sorry. She hugged me and said that she understood. "Bill," she said, "sometimes we get angry when things don't go our way. At times I'm angry about being sick. I wish that I could do as much as I used to do.

None of us likes the way things are right now."

What she said made me feel better. I was glad that Mom and I could talk and share our feelings.

Mom's doctor suggested that our family meet with some other cancer patients and their families. We did. I got to ask a question about something that was really bugging me. I knew cancer wasn't contagious, but I wondered if I would get cancer when I was older. I was told that no one has all the answers about what will happen in the future. What is important is that people are working hard to find a cure for this disease.

I also learned that just because someone in your family has cancer does not mean that you will have it, too. Members of the same family have a greater chance of getting certain types of cancer, but this does not always happen.

I learned that the American Cancer Society has seven warning signs for cancer, which everyone should know about. Mom told me what those signs are in a way that I could understand.

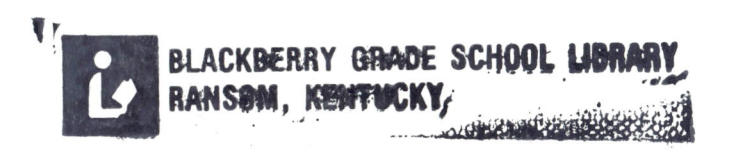

Seven Warning Signs of Cancer

1. Any changes, especially in a bowel movement, when you go to the bathroom
2. A sore throat that doesn't get better
3. Bleeding or drainage from any part of your body
4. A lump or bump or bruise that won't go away
5. Stomach troubles that never stop or difficulty in swallowing
6. A change in the way a wart or mole looks
7. A hoarse voice or cough that won't stop

When cancer is found early, it has a better chance of being controlled. If you have any of the warning signs, ask your parents or another grown-up to take you to a doctor right away. I'm sure glad that my Mom went for her checkup.

Mom's cancer treatments cost a lot of money. Dad said that we had to be more careful with our spending. We cut down on our usual Saturday night pizza. Instead, we made popcorn and played games at home. Sometimes we invited friends to join us. Mom would play when she was feeling well.

Nearly a year has passed. I feel like our family has been on a roller coaster ride. Sometimes I was angry that Mom had cancer. Other times I felt plain scared. Mom is better now, and that makes me happy. I asked if Mom is cured. Her doctor said that she is in remission. Hopefully, her cancer cells will never begin to grow again.

Mom feels very lucky. Not everyone goes into remission. Cancer is a mysterious and terrible disease.

Everything is not just like it was before Mom got sick. We have all learned to do more to help ourselves and each other. I've learned to talk about what is on my mind. The best lesson is that we have all learned to care about each other and make each day count.

Another great happening is that Mom's hair has grown back. She is more beautiful than ever.

Glossary

benign—not malignant; not cancerous

biopsy—a simple operation or special test to remove something from the body so that it can be looked at closely under a microscope

cancer—a disease where cells grow out of control, destroy healthy cells, and threaten life

carcinogen—one of many things that has been shown to cause cancer

cells—tiny parts that help make up the human body

chemical—one of many things that make up matter

chemotherapy—a cancer treatment that uses drugs to destroy cancer cells

contagious—easily spreading from one to another

cure—to free from harm; return to good health

disease—a sickness; an illness

laboratory—a place where scientific work is done

malignant—very harmful; causing death

microscope—an instrument with a lens, which makes tiny objects look larger and easier to see

operation—something done to the body with instruments to improve health or to find out what is wrong

outpatient—someone who goes regularly to the hospital or doctor's office for treatments

radiation—very strong energy that is given off; used in the treatment of cancer to kill cancer cells and prevent the disease from spreading

remission—a word used for cancer that is under control

surgeon—a doctor who performs operations

terminal—a word used for cancer that is out of control and can cause death

tumor—a swelling or lump formed by a buildup of cells; a growth in any part of the body

Adult Resource Guide

Cancer is often a whispered word. The disease is frightening not only to its victims but to many others whose lives can be affected by its seemingly mysterious and destructive nature. When cancer invades a family unit, information and education are a must for helping everyone cope, especially children. Unfortunately, when this disease strikes a parent or other family member, children are often unintentionally forgotten and left to their own imaginations. Too often the results are confusion and unspoken fear. Although *Cancer: The Whispered Word* is in no way intended to be used as a medical guide, we hope this section will help parents and other caring adults communicate with children and deal with the stresses that such an illness entails.

Activity Suggestions for Parents and Children

1. Several cancer support groups are available nationwide. These are for cancer patients and family members. Contact your local American Cancer Society for information.

2. If the child cannot be part of a cancer support group, then an adult who feels comfortable should discuss any of the following questions with the child.
   What questions do you have about cancer?
   What worries you about this illness?
   What things are different because of the cancer illness?
   How do you feel about the changes due to the cancer?
   What is it like having someone close to you ill with cancer?
   Can you think of some things you might be able to do to help yourself? How can you help other people in your family?

3. Have the child begin his or her own book. Any kind of little notebook will do. For fun, cover it with fabric and add cutout letters. Have the child keep track of the things happening in the home. Encourage writing down feelings. The book can be private, or the child may choose to share it with a parent or friend.

4. Continuing to have special family activities is important. Money may be a main concern, so economical outings and entertainment need to be explored. Community parks, churches, schools, city government, and various special interest groups often have fun activities and exhibits. Be sure to check the local newspaper in the leisure or entertainment section for information.

5. Work is never done. There is always plenty to do around the house. Sharing tasks helps everyone. Make up a job chart once a week, and think of a

special reward for the family member who does the best work each week. This can be a special service that other family members provide. Also, be sure to have an **all house** work time once a week. Warn everyone of the day and time in advance. Choose one area of the house where everyone gathers at the same time. Assign a different task to each member, and go to it! For example: living room; dust, vacuum, wash windows, clean drawers, polish accessories, etc. Make working a togetherness time.

6. Cooking responsibilities can be shared by everyone. They also offer a wonderful opportunity for learning new skills. Before children cook, make sure they know basic rules of safety and what to do in emergency situations. Even young children will be able to help.

Easy and nutritious recipes to help out during a stressful time can be found on the following pages.

Easy Cooking

SNACKS

Double Cheese Crisp

2 flour tortillas
Grated cheese

Preheat oven to 350°F. Butter one side of each tortilla. Place one tortilla buttered side down on a cookie sheet. Sprinkle with grated cheese. Place second tortilla on top, buttered side up. Place tortillas in oven until cheese melts. Watch closely!

Dip Sticks

Wash carefully and peel, if necessary, any stick-type vegetables (carrots, celery, zucchini, green pepper, cucumber). Slice and dip in any creamy salad dressing.

Marinated Veggies

Clean vegetables (fresh broccoli, cauliflower, green pepper, zucchini, carrots). Cut into bite size pieces. Place in a deep bowl, and cover with a large bottle of Italian salad dressing. Keep covered in refrigerator, and eat as a snack or with meals as a salad. Drain only the portion you wish to eat. Marinated vegetables will keep for a week.

Great Granola

- 1 pound box 100% natural cereal
- 1 cup dried apples, apricots, or pineapple
- 1 small box raisins
- 1 cup dry roasted peanuts
- 1 cup dry roasted sunflower seeds
- 1 cup chocolate, butterscotch, or carob chips (optional)

Mix ingredients together. Enjoy!

MAIN DISHES

Yummy Chicken

Chicken pieces (use cut-up, whole chicken or favorite parts)
Topping: 1 small jar apricot preserves
          1 package onion soup mix
          1 bottle Russian salad dressing

Wash and pat dry chicken pieces. Place in a large, greased baking dish. Mix together topping ingredients. Pour over chicken. Cover dish with foil and bake at 350°F for 1-1/2 hours.

Crock Pot Beef

1 pound stew meat
1 can cream of mushroom soup
1 package onion soup mix

Place ingredients in crock pot and cook on low all day. Serve with noodles or rice; or add 1 can carrots (drained) and 1 can potatoes (drained). Continue to heat on high for 1 hour.

DESSERTS

Popcorn

After corn is popped, top with Parmesan or other cheese, instead of salt, for a different flavor.

Yogurt Sundae

    Yogurt (any flavor)
    Great granola (see recipe on page 36)

Place alternate layers of yogurt and Great Granola in a goblet or deep dish. Add fresh fruit for a special treat. Top with granola.

About the Authors

Roxane Kunz and Judy Swenson became acquainted in 1969 when they were third grade teachers at the same school. Their common interest in education soon expanded into a close friendship with a variety of shared interests.

Judy's own personal experience with cancer and her training as a support person to cancer patients and their families motivated her to join forces with Roxane to write *Cancer: The Whispered Word*. Roxane, who works full time as a school psychologist and is a certified reality therapist, wanted to provide a realistic, therapeutic, and practical approach to dealing with cancer in families.

Judy and Roxane reside in Arizona. Judy is married and the mother of two boys. Roxane is married and the mother of one grown son. She has a baby grandson.

J
616.994
Swe   Swenson, Judy Harris

Cancer, the whispered word

8792

DATE DUE			
SEP 22			
APR 14			
APR 25			
JAN 7 1991			
OCT 18 1992			

8792

BLACKBERRY GROVE SCHOOL LIBRARY
RANSOM, KENTUCKY